Dear Mother

Mothers Day 2008

with all our love

Barbara and Marion

xx

To

_____

From

_____

Date

_____

A Bouquet for Mother

© 2007 Christian Art Gifts, RSA
        Christian Art Gifts Inc., IL, USA

Artwork © Gail Flores, licensed by Suzanne Cruise
Translated by Linda Beukes

Designed by Christian Art Gifts

Printed in China

ISBN 978-1-86920-754-0

07   08   09   10   11   12   13   14   15   16   –   10   9   8   7   6   5   4   3   2   1

A Bouquet for

Mother

... a sweet fragrance in my life

Nina Smit
Illustrated by Gail Flores

christian
art gifts.

Dedicated
to my mother

I shall never forget my mother,
for it was she who planted
and nurtured the first seeds
of good within me.
She opened my heart
to the impressions of nature;
she awakened my understanding
and extended my horizon,
and her precepts exerted an everlasting
influence upon the course of my life.

~ Immanuel Kant

*It is my mother
who gave me
the gift of life.*

Every mother knows
without a doubt that this
is what she was really
placed on earth for –
to be the bearer of
a brand new life that comes
directly from God.
~ Nina Smit

Thank you, Mother, for carrying me
beneath your heart for nine long –
and often uncomfortable – months,
and that you already started
praying for me then
and cherished dreams about me
for hours on end …

"Can a mother forget the baby
at her breast and have no compassion
on the child she has borne?
Though she may forget, I will not forget you!"
Isaiah 49:15

A *mother* is
God's *love*
in *action*.

~ Anonymous

Thank you, Mother,
for enduring childbirth with a smile;
for loving me irrevocably
and unconditionally
from the first moment that you
held me in your arms.
You have been demonstrating this
selfless love to me
lavishly, from that day onwards.

Who ran to help me when I fell,
And would some pretty story tell,
Or kiss the place to make it well?
My mother.
~ Jane Taylor

As a mother

comforts her child,

so will I comfort you.

Isaiah 66:13

She gets up while it is still dark;
she provides food for her family
and portions for her servant girls.
She sets about her work vigorously;
her arms are strong for her tasks.

Proverbs 31:15, 17

Thank you, Mother,
for getting up for me at night,
for nursing me and for
preparing and cleaning
thousands of bottles
over the next few years.
You taught me to talk
and laugh and walk.
Thank you that I could lay claim
to your love, time and energy
any time of the day or night.

There's no such thing as
a non-working mother.
~ Hester Mundis

Thank you, Mother,
for telling me from the start
that God loves me very much;
that He knows my name
and chose me to be His child.
Thank you for the assurance of knowing
that you pray for me every day.

No man is poor
who has a godly mother.
~ Abraham Lincoln

Arise, cry out in the night,
as the watches of the night begin;
pour out your heart like water
in the presence of the LORD.
Lift up your hands to Him
for the lives of your children.
Lamentations 2:19

Thank you, Mother,
for always praying for me,
and also for teaching me from an early age
that I can talk to God at any time and any place.
That I can praise Him and thank Him
and share my whole life with Him.

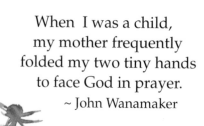

When I was a child,
my mother frequently
folded my two tiny hands
to face God in prayer.
~ John Wanamaker

*"In that day you will no longer ask Me anything.
I tell you the truth, My Father will give you
whatever you ask in My name. Until now
you have not asked for anything in My name. Ask
and you will receive, and your joy will be complete."*
John 16:23-24

I believe the most valuable
contribution a parent
can make to his child
is to instill in him
a genuine faith in God.
~ Dr. James Dobson

The God to whom a little

has a face very much like

boy says his prayers

his mother's. ~ James M. Barrie

19

All that I am I owe to my mother.
I attribute all my success in life
to the moral, intellectual, and physical
education I received from her.
~ George Washington

Thank you, Mother, for telling me
Bible stories when I was small
and for reading from the Children's Bible.
Thank you for nurturing in me
a love for God's Word;
and for buying me my first Holy Bible.

Jesus answered, "It is written: 'Man does not live on bread alone, but on every word that comes from the mouth of God.'"

Matthew 4:4

21

The mother's heart
is the child's schoolroom.
~ Henry Ward Beecher

Thank you, Mother,
for your wisdom
that comes straight from God.
Thank you for teaching me
so many things over the years
and for instilling good values in me.
I have made your life lessons my own,
and it has made me more of the person
God intended me to be.

The fear of the LORD
is the beginning of wisdom,
and knowledge of
the Holy One is understanding.
Proverbs 9:10

*We who have the Spirit
understand these things,
but others can't
understand us at all.*
1 Corinthians 2:15 NLT

Thank you, Mother,
for teaching me the right values.
For impressing on me characteristics
like integrity and honesty,
kindness and faithfulness.
And teaching me that these are the things
that are really important.
These values will guide
my actions for the rest of my life.

When traditional values and wisdom
are ignored, the loss is immeasurable.
From that moment on society
no longer has a compass
to indicate the direction,
and we don't even know
which harbor we are sailing to.
~ Edmund Burke

Thank you, Mother,
for taking care of me so lovingly;
for washing and ironing my clothes,
for cooking my favorite meals,
for helping me with my school work,
for explaining math to me,
and for attending my sports activities.
Thank you for allowing me
to make a mess in your kitchen,
for always having time to listen to me,
for your help and comfort and good advice.

There is no love on earth,
I think, as potent
and enduring as
a mother's love for her child.

~ Ann Kiemel Anderson

*She watches over the affairs
of her household and does not eat
the bread of idleness.
Her children arise and call her blessed;
her husband also, and he praises her.*
Proverbs 31:27-28

Thank you, Mother,
for helping me to know God
and for allowing me to see,
through your example,
how to follow in the
footsteps of the Lord Jesus.
It was how you lived your life
that made me decide
to become a child of God.

Amongst all her possessions,
a mother can only take
her children along with
her to heaven.
~ Anonymous

Here am I, and the children

the LORD *has given me.*

We are signs and symbols

in Israel from the LORD.

Isaiah 8:18

Three words fall sweetly on my soul,
As music from an angel's lyre,
That bids my spirit spurn control,
And upward to its source aspire;
The sweetest sounds to mortals given
Are heard in Mother, Home, and Heaven.

~ William Goldsmith Brown

*The rod of correction
imparts wisdom,
but a child left to himself
disgraces his mother.*

Proverbs 29:15

Without sufficient discipline,
children cannot experience
true security in a family.
All children need boundaries.
Therefore, to give your children love
means that you should also control them
and set clear limits for them.
~ Nina Smit

Thank you, Mother,
for disciplining me,
for clearly teaching me right from wrong,
and where necessary,
setting the right boundaries for me.
Thank you for shaping me into the happy,
well-adjusted adult that I am today.

"Lift up your eyes and look around;
all your sons gather and come to you.
As surely as I live," declares the Lord,
"you will wear them all as ornaments;
you will put them on, like a bride."
Isaiah 49:18

Youth fades; love droops,
the leaves of friendship fall.
A mother's secret love
outlives them all.
~ Oliver Wendell Holmes

Thank you, Mother, for your tremendous
pride in my achievements
even though they weren't extraordinary.
For knowing that you thought I was the best,
the most beautiful,
the cleverest child that ever lived –
although I knew too well
that the opposite was also true!
You taught me to have confidence
in my abilities and instilled in me
a sense of my own worth
because I looked at myself through your eyes.

Thank you, Mother,
for teaching me through the years
that a mother's love –
just like God's love – never changes.
Although everything around me changes,
I know for certain
that you will always love me
because a mother's love is the only love
that can be divided into equal parts
among all her children
and under whose wings a child can find
shelter in all circumstances.

[God] will cover you
with His feathers,
and under His wings
you will find refuge;
His faithfulness will be
your shield and rampart.
Psalm 91:4

A mother's love is a beacon
shining with faith, truth and prayer;
and there her children
find shelter through the
changing scenes of life.
~ Anonymous

This is how God showed His love
among us: He sent His
one and only Son into the world
that we might live through Him.
1 John 4:9

I will never forget the way
we celebrated Christmas –
the Christmas tree
with intriguing gifts under it;
being together,
laughing together,
and the wonderful food.
But my most vivid memory
is of the way you made us
realize what Christmas
is really about –
that it is not a gift festivity
but a celebration of God's love
and the birth of Jesus.

Thank you, Mother!

Sometimes we should become
like children again,
and there is no better time to do
that than at Christmas time,
when the mighty Founder
of the day was a child Himself.

~ Charles Dickens

The greatest value of tradition
is that it gives a family a sense
of identity and belonging.
We all experience the need
to accept that we are a family who live
and breathe and are aware of our uniqueness,
our character and origin.
~ Dr. James Dobson

Mother, I thank you for
upholding so many wonderful family traditions.
Special holidays we celebrated together
and the family traditions
we now teach our children.
I know that these joys were mostly
of your doing and that it was your efforts
that made childhood so special.

Consequently, you are no longer
foreigners and aliens, but
fellow citizens with God's people
and members of God's household.
Ephesians 2:19

As long as she lives, a mother can remain
a foundation to her daughter, and that is what
a good mother should be.
She is the base one always wants to return to,
even when she is no longer there,
because she has become a path finder and guide,
not a chain you want to break free
from as soon as possible.
A righteous, good mother is one
who prays for her children every day;
sometimes a few times a day,
and never stops praying.
And her prayer is not:
Lord make them happy, but:
Lord, make them the reason that
other people are happy.

~ Alba Bouwer

Marriage challenges you
to be the best person
you can possibly be.
And that is why this challenge
is not only exciting but also terrifying.

~ Anonymous

Thank you that I could learn
from you which qualities to look for
in the man I want to spend
the rest of my life with.
I know now that outer appearances
and wealth are worth far less
than caring love, trust in God,
courtesy and faithfulness.
Thanks to you, Mother,
I am happily married now!

"Haven't you read," He replied,
"that at the beginning the Creator
'made them male and female.'"
So they are no longer two, but one.
Therefore what God has joined together,
let man not separate."
Matthew 19:4, 6

*Each one of you also
must love his wife as he
loves himself, and the wife must
respect her husband.*
Ephesians 5:33

Sometimes two people discover each other
and complement each other perfectly.
They learn to be patient
with each other's weaknesses;
cultivate compassion
with each other's irritations;
laugh more than they judge –
for such a love the angels
leave the heavens to sit and sing
from the roof of that house.
~ Francis Schaeffer

Thank you, Mother,
for loving Dad unconditionally
and allowing me to see it.
Your sincere relationship,
the obvious pleasure you found in each other,
and the unselfish way in which
you cherished each other is the main reason
why I am happily married today
and the angels sing from the roof of our house!

Great are the works of the LORD; they are pondered by all who delight in them.
Psalm 111:2

Thank you, Mother,
for radiating inner beauty –
and for teaching me to recognize beauty.
For showing me the sunset clouds
and the dew drops on a spider's web.
For reading poems to me
and for singing and playing music to me.

For when you looked
into my mother's eyes you knew,
as if He had told you,
why God sent her into the world –
it was to open the minds of all
who looked, to beautiful thoughts.
~ James M. Barrie

Train a child
in the way he should go,
and when he is old
he will not turn from it.

Proverbs 22:6

Thank you, Mother,
for bearing with me
through my teenage years;
for loving me despite my
teenage whims and fancies.
For trying to understand
my rebellious spirit
and for allowing me room
to develop my own
personal identity.

When I stopped seeing mother
with the eyes of a child,
I saw the woman who helped me
give birth to myself.

~ Nancy Friday

If I could comfort just one broken heart,
my life would not have been in vain.
If I could alleviate the pain in just one life,
or help one sparrow back into its nest,
my life would not have been in vain.
~ Emily Dickinson

*Carry each other's burdens, and in
this way you will fulfill the law of Christ.*
Galatians 6:2

Thank you, Mother, for always being there
to comfort me when I was sad –
and for still comforting me today.
I can still talk to you about everything
that makes me sad and I know that I
will feel much better after speaking to you.

My mother was a builder, an architect with plans for a better tomorrow. Her foundation was laid on pure goodness. Her walls were built with exceptional life art.

The windows could open up widely for love and understanding. A roof of faith protected her house against the storms of life. A wall of contentment kept out strife, prejudice and resentment.

She had not merely built a house, it was a home where the heart could find rest.

~ Beulah Squires

The place where you reign
is more than just four walls and a roof –
it is a home where you create
an oasis of love, happiness
and safety for your loved ones.
~ Nina Smit

Thank you, Mother, for making
our house a true home;
for creating a loving atmosphere
of warmth and life.
For always being finely tuned
into each person's needs
so that not only our family –
but also other relatives, guests and friends
who came to visit us
could feel the love
and feel happy and at home.

*Therefore encourage one another
and build each other up,
just as in fact you are doing.*
1 Thessalonians 5:11

A woman's heart determines
how she thinks and behaves
and it influences to a great extent
the atmosphere of her home
as well as the characters
of her children.

~ Elise Grey

Thank you, dear Mother,
for making our house
such a wonderful place to grow up in –
a place where my friends
were always welcome.
A home filled with fresh flowers,
exquisite paintings, books
and beautiful music –
even though it might not have been
scrupulously tidy every day.
A home where every guest could clearly
feel the happiness of those living there.

Listen to your father, who gave you life,
and do not despise your mother when she is old.
Proverbs 23:22

Thank you, Mother, for always
making time for me, even when
you were very busy.
For making time
when there really wasn't any time;
for always being there for me and
for allowing me to talk to you
about anything at any time.
For being a "story mom" who told me
the most wonderful stories
from a very early age –
this has created a deep love for literature in me.

Whatever your hand finds to do,
do it with all your might, for in the grave,
where you are going, there is neither working
nor planning nor knowledge nor wisdom.
Ecclesiastes 9:10

Thank you, Mother,
for accepting me exactly the way I am;
for never trying to change me
into a valedictorian or super sports star;
for being quite happy with the plain old me.
Thank you for never expecting more from me
than what I could be or give
and for allowing me to know
that my best was entirely good enough for you.

Make an effort from now
on to give your children
the freedom to express
their individuality within
the safety of your family.

~ Nina Smit

Accept one another,
then, just as Christ accepted you,
in order to bring praise to God.
Romans 15:7

Thank you, Mother, for introducing me
to the wonderful world of books
even before I could read on my own.
Thank you for all the amazing books you gave me.
I am most thankful for the fact
that you introduced me to
the most amazing book of all time:
the Word of God – still the light of my life.

Books can make the poorest man rich.
They bring about a kind of wealth
that nothing on earth can take away from you.
They offer you friends that never fail you.
They provide pleasure that never ceases.
~ Eugene Bertin

*Take the helmet of salvation and
the sword of the Spirit, which is the word of God.
And pray in the Spirit on all occasions with
all kinds of prayers and requests. With this in mind,
be alert and always keep on praying for all the saints.*
Ephesians 6:17-18

A mother's love for her child is
like no other love you will find.
It burns with such a bright,
constant flame that it seems to be
the one unchangeable thing in this fickle life.
When a mother is no longer there, she
remains a light for our footsteps and a comfort.
~ W. D. Hudson

My mother's love for me
was so great that I had
to work very hard for
my entire life to justify it.
~ Marc Chagall

Thank you, Mother,
for personally demonstrating selfless love
to us in our home every day.
We learned first hand of a love
that is patient and kind, that does not envy
or keep a record of wrongs.
A love that always protects,
always trusts and always perseveres.
A love that is willing to forgive
over and over again.
You have set me an example
that I will struggle to match.

*We were gentle
among you, like a
mother caring
for her little children.*

1 Thessalonians 2:7

63

Knowledge is joy, because having knowledge –
insightful, thorough knowledge –
means being able to distinguish
between true and false and
between good and bad things.

~ Anonymous

Thank you, Mother, for teaching me
from an early age that knowledge is power,
for clearly explaining to me –
and for underlining it in the Bible –
the difference between right and wrong,
so that I knew exactly how to live
when reaching adulthood.
I can now pass that same
knowledge on to my children.

My son, pay attention to my wisdom,
listen well to my words of insight,
that you may maintain discretion
and your lips may preserve knowledge.
Proverbs 5:1-2

For surely, O LORD,
You bless the righteous; You surround them
with Your favor as with a shield.

Psalm 5:12

God truly wants you to show your trust
in Him by going through life with a smile.
And when you really think about it,
you have reason to smile: you are in the
hands and under the direction of
the almighty God and Father who
loves you and delights in blessing you.
~ Johan Smit

Thank you, Mother,
for teaching me to find joy
in everyday things;
to take nothing for granted,
but always to be grateful
towards God and other people.
To be optimistic and cheerful
in all circumstances
so that other people can see
God's joy in my life.

Thank you, Mother, for allowing me
to be independent; for allowing me
to dream my own dreams
and follow my own heart.
For helping me to experience the sharp edges
of life as a learning opportunity –
and for never tying me to
your apron strings and
for never trying to run my life.

Your mother's house is the place
where you can go –
whether you are sixteen or sixty –
to show off when the world
carries you on its shoulders
and to cry when
it tramples you under its feet,
because you know
there they will not take
your importance too seriously,
and if you have made a mistake,
they will not stop loving you.

~ Anonymous

A mother is not a person
to lean on, but a person
to make leaning unnecessary.

~ Dorothy Canfield Fisher

Children are a gift from the LORD,
they are a reward from Him.

Psalm 127:3 NLT

*Whoever claims to live in Him
must walk as Jesus did.*
1 John 2:6

My mother taught me that God
does not live in churches
that we only visit on Sundays,
like a relative who is ill.
She showed me a God
who lives in the present
and who listens to my prayers,
treats me with sympathy
and who, at the end of the day,
will hold me accountable:
to my parents and to Him.

~ Jill Briscoe

Thank you, Mother, for showing me
every day what God looks like –
and how Jesus wants His children to live.
Thank you for really practicing your faith.
I can see the actions and words
of Jesus through your life.
Because I have you as an example
I sometimes succeed
in following in your footsteps.

Thank you, Mother, for supporting me
in the things I did; for being on my side
when Dad needed to be convinced
to buy me a new dress or a new pair of shoes,
and for asking permission on my behalf
when I wanted to stay out a little longer than usual ...
Thank you, Mother, for your unconditional trust
in me which has encouraged me
to make a success of my life.

The mother loves her child most divinely,
not when she surrounds him
with comfort and anticipates his wants,
but when she resolutely holds him
to the highest standards and is
content with nothing less than his best.
~ Hamilton Wright Mabie

*The righteous man
leads a blameless life;
blessed are his
children after him.*

Proverbs 20:7

Thank you so much, Mother,
for teaching me the meaning
of honesty, sincerity and integrity.
And for practicing these qualities in your life.
Thank you that I could always
trust your word because you always
keep your promises and don't hesitate
to apologize when you are wrong.
That things are well with all your children today
is mostly thanks to you!

As the Spirit of the Lord works within us,
we become more and more like Him
and reflect His glory even more.
2 Corinthians 3:18 NLT

The word 'integrity' is about wholeness
and therefore also honesty and sincerity.
In the life of a person with integrity
certain things are not at odds.
He or she does not pretend to be
what they are not, or say something
they do not really mean.
Integrity is transparency, frankness.
Just like it was made visible in the life of Jesus.
~ F. W. Robertson

Now that I have children of my own,
I realize for the first time how much
you really did for me,
how much you sacrificed
without my even realizing it,
how much you loved me
and all the different ways in which
you showed me your love
without my even noticing it.
It is only now that I discover
how many times your love guided me
in the right direction.
Thank you, Mother!

Where there is
a mother in the house,
matters speed well.
~ Amos Alcott

A wife of noble character who can find?
She is worth far more than rubies. She is clothed
with strength and dignity; she can laugh at
the days to come. She speaks with wisdom,
and faithful instruction is on her tongue.
Proverbs 31:10, 25-26

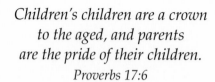

*Children's children are a crown
to the aged, and parents
are the pride of their children.*
Proverbs 17:6

Nobody can do
for little children
what grandparents do.
Grandparents sort of sprinkle
stardust over the lives
of little children.
~ Alex Haley

Thank you, Mother,
for being the best grandmother
any child could wish for –
for revelling in the joy
of having grandchildren.
Thank you that my children
are so privileged to be
on the receiving end of such
a wonderful grandmother's love,
and that they may
have so much fun with you.
Thank you for telling them
the same stories that you told me
and for telling them
the same things you taught me.

Now that you are old, Mother,
it is my turn to pay you back,
with interest, for all the love
and care I received from you
all these years.
Thank you, Mother,
for allowing me to do this.

It makes no difference how old you are,
in the essence of every person
there is the love of miracles,
the fearless challenges
of opportunities and the joy of life.

~ Douglas MacArthur

May the LORD bless you from
Zion all the days of your life;
may you see the prosperity of Jerusalem,
and may you live to see your children's
children. Peace be upon Israel.

Psalm 128:5-6

Holy as heaven a mother's tender love,
the love of many prayers and
many tears which changes
not with dim, declining years.

~ Caroline Norton

*My mother brings
sunshine into the house;
it is a pleasure to be there.*

~ Cecil Beaton

Thank you, Mother,
for being a sunshine mom
who transformed our house
into a sunshine home
and brought light into our lives.
Even though I know you
will not always be there,
I will always carry the precious memory
of your warmth and loving care with me.

For God, who said,
"Let light shine out of darkness,"
made His light shine in our hearts
to give us the light of the knowledge
of the glory of God in the face of Christ.
2 Corinthians 4:6